*For William*

*Composer's World*

# Wolfgang Amadeus Mozart

*by Wendy Thompson*

VIKING

# Introduction

Many people consider Wolfgang Amadeus Mozart to be the greatest composer the world has ever known. In his short lifetime – he died aged only thirty-five – he wrote a huge amount of music in every form and style of his day, ranging from operas to symphonies, concertos, chamber music, piano music, songs, and church music. In spite of the amazing speed at which he worked, hardly any of Mozart's music shows signs of haste or carelessness: it is all of high quality.

Mozart's career was shaped by the circumstances under which he lived. He was born at a time when Europe was ruled by mighty dynasties – the Romanovs in Russia, the Bourbons in France, the Hanoverians in England, and the powerful Hapsburgs in Mozart's own Austria. Elsewhere, in the collection of states known as Germany, for instance, a motley assortment of lesser princes ruled over their own little empires. The "middle classes" – professional people as we know them – hardly existed, while the majority still worked for the aristocracy, as servants or laborers. Musicians, and especially composers, occupied a peculiar place in this hierarchy: many worked for the courts, and instead of being treated with reverence as creative artists, they were regarded (and regarded themselves) as craftsmen, doing a specific job as required for a sum of money.

Mozart was one of the first composers who tried to break free from the shackles of patronage, and establish a career in his own right, working as a "freelance." As we shall see, the time was not yet right for such a bold venture, and it was not a success, which contributed to his early death. But apart from his unique gifts as a composer, which have ensured the survival of his music, Mozart's independent spirit "broke the mold" of the old view of the composer as servant, and helped to raise the status of the artist in society.

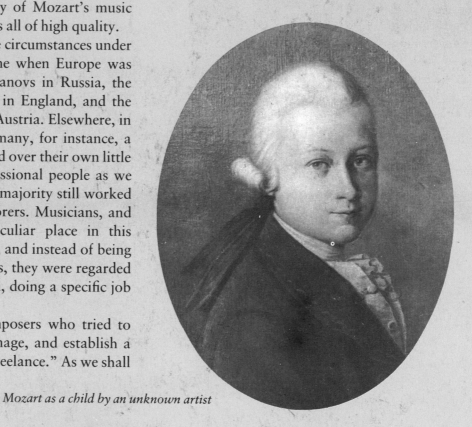

*Mozart as a child by an unknown artist*

# 1 Childhood: The Traveller

Wolfgang Amadeus Mozart was born on January 27, 1756 in the picturesque town of Salzburg, in the Austrian Alps. His father, Leopold Mozart, worked as a violinist in the court orchestra of the Archbishop of Salzburg, the most important person in the town. In those days, making a living as a musician was a precarious business, and almost all players and composers worked for a patron – a monarch such as Frederick the Great of Prussia or the Empress Maria Theresia of Austria; a nobleman such as Prince Esterházy, who employed the great composer Joseph Haydn; or a dignitary of the Church, such as the Archbishop of Salzburg. Such a post was secure – so long as the patron was kept

*The house where Mozart was born*

*A view of Salzburg in Mozart's time*

happy – but it was very restricting: the musicians were treated as no better than servants, and were expected to be constantly at their master's beck and call. They were also expected to write music to order: if Prince Esterházy wanted a new symphony to entertain his guests in a week's time, poor Haydn had to produce one by that date – and no excuses were allowed!

By 1757 Leopold Mozart was becoming quite well known in a modest way. He had published an important manual on violin playing, and the Archbishop had appointed him court and chamber composer. His wife, Anna Maria, was a cheerful, homely Salzburger – not particularly bright, but a good housekeeper and a devoted wife and mother. Altogether they had seven children; but, like many families at this time, they lost several either at birth or during childhood. Growing up was a dangerous affair in days when there were no antibiotics to cure fatal illnesses such as smallpox and scarlet fever. Only one of the Mozart children, a girl named Maria Anna (Nannerl for short) was still alive when little Wolfgang – the "miracle God let be born in Salzburg" – arrived four and a half years later.

Nannerl began to learn the piano when she was seven, and quickly showed that she was very talented. But her little brother started to teach himself some of Nannerl's pieces, and at the age of only four, he had even begun to compose some himself, with his father's help. Leopold was soon convinced that he had a child prodigy – a genius – on his hands, and he was determined that the world should know of it. In the eighteenth and nineteenth centuries, child prodigies were the equivalent of today's pop stars: they toured around, giving concerts, while people flocked to hear them and showered them with gifts of money and jewels. Leopold Mozart saw nothing wrong with exploiting his son's talents in that way – indeed, he saw it as his duty to

*Leopold Mozart (1719–1787)*

promote Wolfgang's career, and to secure the family's financial future. "God, who has been far too good to a sinner like me, has blessed my children with such talent, that, apart from my duty as a father, this fact alone would encourage me to devote myself only to their successful development." So, when Wolfgang was six and Nannerl eleven, he took them first to Munich where they played to the Elector of Bavaria, and then to Vienna, approximately 150 miles away, where they were received by the Empress Maria Theresia at the beautiful Schönbrunn Palace. She was so delighted with

## Wolfgang's first piece, written around his fifth birthday

*The palace of Schönbrunn, in the 18th century, and today*

*A View of the Palace and Gardens of Schonbrun built by his Imperial Majesty Joseph 1.st for a Hunting Seat*

the children that she gave each of them a magnificent set of court clothes, which they wore for a special portrait. Wolfgang himself caused a great deal of amusement, and some embarrassment to his parents, by cheekily proposing marriage to the Empress's six-year-old daughter, Marie Antoinette – the future Queen of France.

*Wolfgang aged 7, in court dress*

*Leopold Mozart, Nannerl and Wolfgang*

6

*An early Minuet by Wolfgang, written at the time of his sixth birthday*

*Wolfgang giving a concert at the Prince de Conti's tea party in Paris*

By the time Wolfgang was seven, he could compose music as he played it, without having to write it down first. He was expert at this improvisation on the keyboard in all sorts of styles, could play with the keys hidden under a cloth, sight-read anything he was given, however difficult, and had taught himself the violin. He also had "perfect pitch" — which meant he could sing any note without having to hear it first; and he once astonished a family friend by remembering that there was a tiny, but noticeable difference in the tuning of their two violins, even though it was weeks since he had heard the friend's fiddle.

By this time, Leopold had more ambitious plans for his exceptional children. In June 1763 the whole family set out for Paris and England — a long, wearisome, and dangerous journey then. They travelled by stagecoach, stopping off at larger towns and cities along the way to play for the local aristocracy. But not much money came their way, to Leopold's disgust; instead they built up quite a collection of snuffboxes! In Paris, they were introduced to the French court at the vast and splendid Palace of Versailles, and were allowed to watch the royal family at a state banquet: the Queen petted Wolfgang and fed him morsels from her plate, like a little dog. "At present, four sonatas of M. Wolfgang Mozart are being engraved," wrote Leopold proudly to his

landlord in Salzburg. "Imagine the stir they will make when people find out they have been composed by a seven-year-old. God performs new miracles every day through this child."

From Paris, the Mozarts crossed the Channel over to London, where George III and his German wife Charlotte had recently been crowned King and Queen. Both the King and Queen loved music, and the Mozarts were made to feel most welcome. "On April 27th we were with the King and Queen in the Queen's Palace in St James' Park," reported Leopold. "The graciousness with which both Their Majesties received us cannot be described. Their easy manner and friendliness made us forget that they were the King and Queen of England."

Music flourished everywhere in the London of the 1760s — in the theaters, at court, in the concert rooms, and in the great pleasure gardens, where people spent their leisure hours eating, strolling down the leafy alleys, watching firework displays and listening to open-air concerts. Wolfgang played one of his own compositions at Ranelagh Gardens, and also appeared at court, where he delighted George III by playing pieces by the royal favorite, Handel, and accompanying the Queen when she sang a song. To

Leopold's joy, the English proved more generous than the stingy French, and showed their appreciation in hard cash, rather than snuffboxes. Wolfgang quickly made friends with the best and most popular composer then working in London, Johann Christian Bach, the youngest son of the great Johann Sebastian Bach. Johann Christian spent many hours playing duets with young Wolfgang, who was careful to study the way Bach put his music together. The family spent part of their time in Ebury Street, in Chelsea (which was then practically in the country), and the house where they stayed (No. 180) is still there. "It has a lovely garden and one of the most beautiful views in the world," wrote Leopold. "Wherever I look, I see only greenery and in the distance the most splendid castles." Sadly this view has now been replaced by a block of flats; but it was there that Wolfgang composed his first symphonies, in the style of his friend J.C. Bach.

But although the children were a great success, the family did not make as much money in London as Leopold would have liked. "After several sleepless nights I have decided that I will not bring my children up in such a dangerous place, where most people are godless and where one sees such terrible examples," wrote Leopold. "You would be amazed if you saw how children are brought up here."

So the Mozarts decided to leave London. They travelled back to Salzburg via northern France and the Netherlands, where both children fell dangerously ill with typhoid fever. Nannerl nearly died. Wolfgang recovered enough to give two concerts in Amsterdam where one of his new symphonies was heard. After another visit to Paris, they finally arrived home at the end of November 1766. "When we get home, nobody will recognise little Wolfgang," wrote his father from Paris. "It's a long time since we left, and meanwhile he has seen and got to know thousands of people."

*Ranelagh Gardens in the 18th century*

*No. 180 Ebury Street,
where the Mozarts stayed*

# 2 On the Road again — Vienna and Italy

After only nine months at home, Leopold decided to take his family to Vienna, where a great celebration was to take place for the wedding of an Austrian archduchess. But just as they arrived, the bride-to-be died in a smallpox epidemic, and the city was plunged into mourning. Fearing for his children's safety, Leopold hastily withdrew them to a town in what is now Czechoslovakia – but too late. Both Nannerl and Wolfgang were found to have caught the dreaded disease, but fortunately only mildly. Nevertheless, Wolfgang's childish good looks were marred forever by pockmarks.

Once the epidemic was over, the Mozarts returned to Vienna, where Leopold was determined to persuade the Emperor to allow Wolfgang to write an opera for the court. No composer of the time was considered worthy of the name until he had written an opera – then thought to be the highest form of musical achievement. "The Viennese, in general don't want to see serious and thoughtful performances, they only want to see silly stuff – dances, devils, ghosts, magic, clowns, witches," wrote Leopold bitterly. But, although the Emperor seemed to be in favor of the idea, Wolfgang was to encounter his first taste of professional jealousy. A powerful clique of composers and musicians associated with the court were determined not to be outshone by a mere child, and they used their influence to prevent the opera from being commissioned. "I was told that all the performers and composers in Vienna were opposed to our progress – everyone tried most carefully to avoid seeing us and acknowledging little Wolfgang's skill," wrote his disappointed father. But there was a consolation prize: Wolfgang's little musical play, *Bastien and Bastienne*, was put on privately at the house of Dr. Mesmer (who invented mesmerism, or hypnotism), and he was asked to conduct in front of the Imperial court a Mass that he had written. Then

*A view of Vienna today*

*A view of Vienna in the 18th century*

teen her concert-giving days were over, since she was now too old to be considered a child prodigy.) By the end of January 1770 they had reached Milan, where they met several important composers. "Praise God we are both well," wrote Leopold to his anxious wife back in Salzburg. "Wolfgang will certainly not spoil his health by over-eating – I've never seen him take so much care of himself as he does here. Often he doesn't eat much, but nevertheless he is fat and cheerful and jolly all day long." "Here I am," wrote Mozart to his sister in the eighteenth-century equivalent of a postcard. "I kiss Mamma's hands a thousand times and send you a hundred kisses or slaps on your great horseface." The next stop was Bologna, where Wolfgang was "examined" by the famous musical theorist Padre Martini – he passed all Martini's difficult tests with flying colors. Then they visited

when he returned home to Salzburg, he set about writing the opera anyway – a comic piece called *La finta semplice* (The apparent idiot), and it was performed at the Archbishop's palace on May 1, 1769. Wolfgang was rewarded with the honorary title of *Konzertmeister.*

Leopold was soon restless again. He wanted to take Wolfgang to Italy, the land where culture – and especially music – reigned supreme. Italian was the universal language for music (indeed, modern musical terms are still generally given in Italian), and nearly all operas were sung in Italian. Every young European wanted to visit Italy, and the Grand Tour – which all upper-class young men were expected to undertake when they became twenty-one – took in the obligatory sights of Florence, Rome, the ruins of Pompeii, and the Bay of Naples.

Leopold and Wolfgang set out for Italy in December 1769, leaving Nannerl at home with her mother. (At eigh-

*Padre Martini (1706–1784)*

11

*Wolfgang as a Knight of the Golden Spur*

*Thomas Linley (1756–1778), painted by Gainsborough*

**1776**

Florence, where Wolfgang met the young English violinist, Thomas Linley, another "child prodigy" of his own age, who was also to die tragically young (he was drowned at twenty-two). The two boys got on amazingly well, and young Thomas "wept bitterly" when they had to part.

In Florence, Wolfgang was invited to play for the Grand Duke. "We were taken to the castle outside the town where we stayed until after ten o' clock," wrote Leopold to his wife and daughter. "Everything went off as usual, and everyone was quite astonished as the Director of Music, who is the greatest expert in counterpoint in all Italy, placed the most difficult fugues before Wolfgang and gave him the most difficult themes, which he threw off and worked out as easily as eating a piece of cake."

The Mozarts spent Easter in Rome, where Wolfgang astonished everyone by writing down from memory a famous choral piece – Allegri's *Miserere* – which he had heard only once in the Sistine Chapel. Then they went on to Naples, where they were received by the King and Queen, went to the opera, and visited the sights. "We saw the King and Queen at Mass in the court chapel at Portici, and we have seen Vesuvius too," wrote Wolfgang to Nannerl.

OLFGANGO MOZART ACCAD.

"Naples is beautiful, but it is just as crowded as Vienna and Paris, and the people are even ruder here than they are in London." Leopold was most disappointed with the famous volcano: "Vesuvius has not yet obliged me by appearing to burn or spit fire. Sometimes you see a puff of smoke . . ."

"I'm still alive and as happy as usual and I just love travelling," wrote Wolfgang enthusiastically. "I've now been on the 'Merditerranean' too. I kiss Mamma's hand and Nannerl 1000 times and am your Dum-Dum of a son and Jack Prat of a brother."

Back in Rome, Wolfgang was made a Knight of the Order of the Golden Spur by the Pope – a very high honor – and he was painted wearing his medal. "Wolfgang has been given a beautiful gold cross to wear . . . you can imagine how I laugh when I hear people calling him 'Signor Cavaliere' all the time," wrote Leopold. Further honors awaited him at Bologna, where he passed the difficult entrance exam for membership of the famous Accademia Filarmonica. He had to compose an intricate piece (in a locked room, to prevent cheating), and finished the job, which took some composers four hours, in just under an hour.

Meanwhile, Wolfgang was growing up fast. He was now fourteen and his voice had broken. "I shall have to have nearly all Wolfgang's clothes altered," wrote Leopold to his wife. "Everything he wears is too tight – his limbs are becoming bigger and stronger. He now has neither a low nor a high voice . . . it makes him cross that he can no longer sing his own pieces." Father and son went back to Milan, where Wolfgang had been asked to write an opera for the court. *Mitridate, re di Ponto* (Mithridates, king of Pontus) was composed and rehearsed during the autumn of 1770, and was first performed on Boxing Day with great success. "After all the arias, except a few at the end, there was much applause and cries of 'Evivva il Maestro! Evviva il Maes-

*The theater in Milan where two of Wolfgang's early operas were performed*

trino!'" reported Leopold. To Wolfgang's delight, another opera was immediately commissioned, together with an oratorio for Padua and a festive piece for the forthcoming wedding celebrations of Maria Theresia's son, the Archduke Ferdinand (then ruler of Milan). After a short period at home, Wolfgang and his father returned to Milan in August 1771 for the wedding, and Wolfgang's piece was once more well received. But when he asked for a job with the Archduke, he was turned down – the first of many such snubs. The Empress had advised her son not to burden himself with such "useless people" as the Mozarts. Ten months later, they visited Italy for the third and last time for the performance of the new opera, *Lucio Silla* (about an ancient Roman Emperor). It, too, was a great success, but once again, Leopold's request for a job for his son was turned down. Disillusioned, the Mozarts returned home.

*Archbishop Hieronymus Colloredo (1732–1812)*

There, circumstances had changed a great deal. Old Archbishop Schrattenbach had died, and a new one had taken his place. Schrattenbach had been a kindly and indulgent employer, willing to give Leopold extended periods of leave to travel with his family, but the new Archbishop was very different. Hieronymus Colloredo was a cold, intolerant, and austere man, very conscious of his own exalted status, and of the humble positions occupied by his servants. Although he had formally confirmed Wolfgang's job as *Konzertmeister*, on a salary of 150 florins a year (about $25 then, or $500 in today's money – not much, but the cost of living in Austria then was very cheap), Leopold was seriously worried about his son's career. He felt that the new Archbishop would not appreciate Wolfgang's exceptional talent. So, as soon as Colloredo's back was turned, Leopold sneaked Wolfgang off to Vienna, hoping to get him a job at the court. But no appointment was forthcoming. "Her Majesty the Empress was very gracious to us, but that

*St Peter's Church, Salzburg*

*Joseph Haydn (1732–1809), painted by Thomas Hardy*

(The gardener in disguise) for Munich, which he and Leopold visited in January 1775 for the first performance: it was the last trip they would take together. "My opera was performed yesterday for the first time and was such a success that I couldn't possibly describe the applause," wrote Wolfgang to his mother. "The whole theatre was so full that many people had to be turned away. Then after each aria there was a terrific noise – hands clapping and cries of 'Viva Maestro!' Afterwards I went with Papa to a room through which the Elector and the whole court had to pass, and I kissed the hands of the Elector and Electress who were very gracious . . . I fear we cannot come home very soon, and Mamma must not wish it, for she knows how much good it does me to feel free."

After having much made of him by the powerful Elector of Bavaria, Mozart felt humiliated by his lowly position at provincial, boring Salzburg: he wanted excitement, glamor, and fame. But in the meantime, he bided his time and continued to compose more music: five violin concertos, four impressive new piano concertos, and several light entertainment pieces, including the famous "Haffner" Serenade for the wedding of a Salzburg merchant's daughter.

was it." However, Wolfgang did make some valuable contacts, especially with the music of Joseph Haydn, the most important and successful European composer of his day. Haydn had just published an exciting and original set of string quartets, and Wolfgang enthusiastically set to work straight away to write a similar set. Haydn's music was to be a continual inspiration for Mozart's later work, and the two composers became close friends, often playing chamber music together.

Wolfgang spent the rest of 1773 and most of 1774 at home, writing eight symphonies, in which his style gradually matured, his first original piano concerto (a form he was to develop almost single-handedly), and a good deal of sacred music for use at Salzburg Cathedral. In the summer of 1774 he was asked to write a comic opera, *La finta giardiniera*

*Salzburg today*

*The slow movement of Mozart's first original piano concerto,*
*written in 1773 when he was 17*

17

In August 1777, Wolfgang decided that he had had enough of the Archbishop, and asked to be released. Colloredo, who saw him only as a troublemaker, was happy to agree, and Wolfgang promptly set out on yet another tour, this time with his mother, since Leopold could not get permission for another long period of leave.

This was the first time that Wolfgang had been anywhere without his fussy and domineering father, and he was glad to be free. He was now twenty-one and, so far, he had devoted his entire life to music. Now he wanted to enjoy himself. After stopping at Munich to play to the Elector, Mozart and his mother went on to Augsburg, where his father had relatives. There, Wolfgang met his lively young cousin, Anna Maria Thekla, with whom he carried on a mild flirtation and an exchange of rather smutty letters in a private joky language, signing himself "your little piggy-wiggy, Wolfgang Amade Silly Billy!" "My little cousin is pretty, bright, charming, clever and gay," wrote Wolfgang to Leopold. "We get on really well, for, like myself, she is a bit of a rascal. We both laugh at everyone and have a good time." Leopold was not amused. "If you want to live in Paris, you must adopt quite a different way of carrying on and a very different outlook," he sternly told his son. "You must devote all your attention to earning some money and you must cultivate a respectful manner in order to ingratiate yourself with people who matter . . . you should have more important things to think about than practical jokes, or you'll suddenly find yourself up the creek. Where there is no money, friends can no longer be found." Unrepentant, Wolfgang wrote to his sister, "I can't write anything sensible today as I rails off the am quite. Papa cross not be must. I that just like today feel. I help it cannot. Bood-gye. I gish you

nood-wight. Sound sleeply. Next time sensible I'll more writely!"

But soon he received orders from Leopold to travel on to Mannheim, one of the most important musical centres of Europe. In this elegant city on the banks of the Rhine, the Elector Palatine had built himself a magnificent palace, with a beautiful opera house, and one of the best and most highly disciplined orchestras that could be found anywhere – "an army of generals," as the English historian Dr. Burney called it. The Elector himself was a great music-lover, and demanded a constant feast of music – operas, symphony concerts, and chamber music recitals.

Wolfgang took to the cultured atmosphere like a duck to water. He immediately made friends with several players in the orchestra – Christian Cannabich, the leader, the

*Mannheim in the 1770s*

*Mozart giving Aloysia Weber a singing lesson*

flautist Wendling and the oboist Ramm. In a rather unwise letter to Leopold, Wolfgang described how he enjoyed riotous evenings at Cannabich's house, making up rude verses and staying up until after midnight. Leopold, naturally, was displeased. Wolfgang appeared to be wasting his time and his talent, and falling into bad company. And still he had failed to get a permanent job. Then, an even worse disaster (from Leopold's point of view) happened. Wolfgang fell madly in love – with a young singer called Aloysia Weber. He was completely swept off his feet, and even proposed abandoning his own tour in order to take Aloysia to Italy to establish her career. Leopold wrote a furious letter to his son. "The purpose of your journey was either to get a good permanent appointment, or failing that, to go off to some big city where you could earn lots of money. Both plans were intended to help your parents and your dear sister, but above all, to establish your own name and reputation. But now, as for your proposal to travel about with Herr Weber and – let it be said – his two daughters, it has nearly made me go mad! How could you let yourself be taken in by such a dreadful idea? Your letter reads like a fairytale!"

Leopold angrily ordered his errant son onwards to his destination – Paris – where he was to "take his place among great men." "Millions have not received the great gift which God has bestowed on you. What a responsibility! And what a tragedy if so great a genius were to sink without trace!" Thoroughly miserable, Wolfgang sullenly dragged himself away from Mannheim and Aloysia on March 14, 1778, reaching Paris (after a wretched journey) ten days later.

He arrived in the middle of a seething cauldron of political and artistic turmoil. The little girl to whom Wolfgang had impudently proposed marriage fifteen years earlier was now Louis XVI's Queen, and her extravagant lifestyle was the subject of much discontented gossip. Just over a decade later, she, her family, and most of France's aristocracy and intellectuals were to lose their heads in Europe's bloodiest Revolution. But meanwhile it was business as usual with the upper classes, who spent their days and nights gambling, hunting, and dancing; the bourgeoisie, led by writers such as Voltaire and Diderot, were busy trying to reform society; while the poor were being told to eat cake, if they had no bread.

The musical world, too, was bitterly divided by a fierce argument between supporters of traditional French opera (a stilted, formal, and outdated type of entertainment), and those who preferred the new, more realistic Italian style. Circumstances were not very favorable for a relatively unknown Austrian composer to make his mark, however

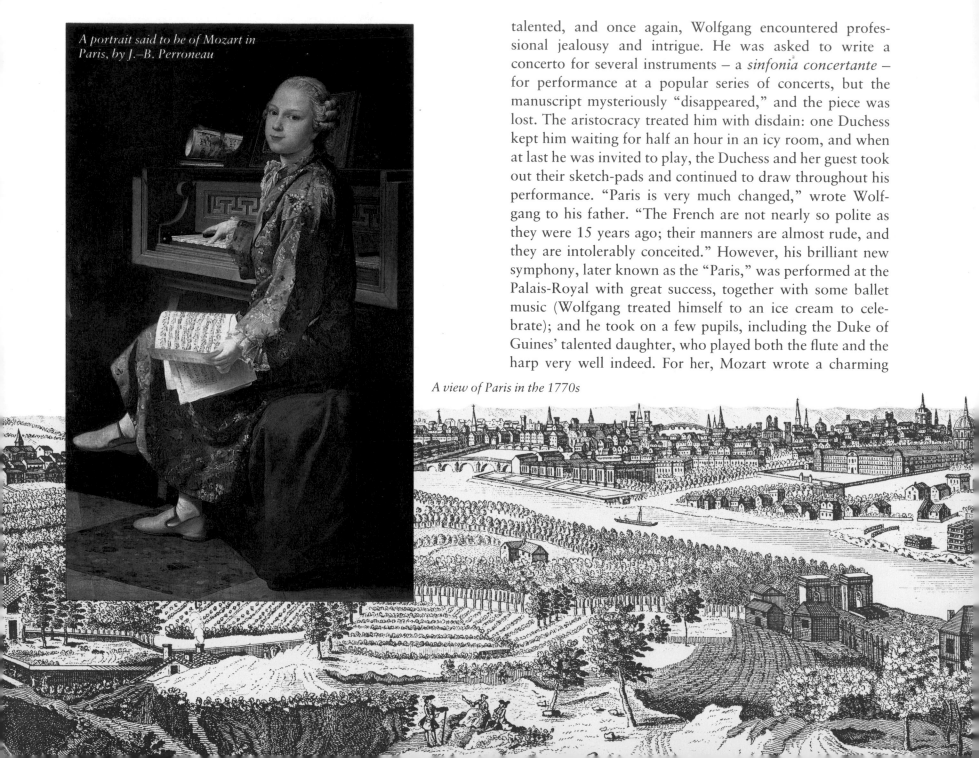

A portrait said to be of Mozart in Paris, by J.–B. Perroneau

talented, and once again, Wolfgang encountered professional jealousy and intrigue. He was asked to write a concerto for several instruments – a *sinfonia concertante* – for performance at a popular series of concerts, but the manuscript mysteriously "disappeared," and the piece was lost. The aristocracy treated him with disdain: one Duchess kept him waiting for half an hour in an icy room, and when at last he was invited to play, the Duchess and her guest took out their sketch-pads and continued to draw throughout his performance. "Paris is very much changed," wrote Wolfgang to his father. "The French are not nearly so polite as they were 15 years ago; their manners are almost rude, and they are intolerably conceited." However, his brilliant new symphony, later known as the "Paris," was performed at the Palais-Royal with great success, together with some ballet music (Wolfgang treated himself to an ice cream to celebrate); and he took on a few pupils, including the Duke of Guines' talented daughter, who played both the flute and the harp very well indeed. For her, Mozart wrote a charming

*A view of Paris in the 1770s*

double concerto in which she could choose to play either instrument.

But then, tragedy struck. Wolfgang's mother, who had had to spend her time in Paris sitting alone in a little dark room where she could not see the sun, suddenly fell ill, and, in spite of all attempts to save her, she died within a few days. Wolfgang hardly knew how to break the news to his father. Desperate to get his beloved son back to Salzburg, Leopold pleaded with the Archbishop to reinstate Wolfgang. Most surprisingly, the Archbishop agreed to have him back, and on greatly improved terms – including a large pay rise, and the opportunity of leave when he wanted it. Wolfgang clearly had no choice but to accept. He was only too glad to leave Paris, which he hated; but before going home, he wanted to see Aloysia again. So he eagerly set off – on a slow, cheap coach, since he had very little money left – to Mannheim, where bitter disappointment awaited him. While Wolfgang was in Paris, the Elector Palatine had become Elector of the whole of Bavaria, and had moved himself and his entourage to the Bavarian capital of Munich. Wearily, Wolfgang set off for Munich in pursuit of Aloysia, only to find that she had changed her mind, and was no longer interested in him. There was nothing for it but to return home to Salzburg, without his mother or his girlfriend. He arrived home just before his twenty-third birthday, in January 1779. It must have been a sad homecoming.

As before, Wolfgang tried to bury his disappointment in work, writing several more symphonies, the "Posthorn" Serenade, a double piano concerto for himself and his sister to play, and the lovely *Sinfonia concertante* for violin and viola. As part of his official duties at Salzburg Cathedral, he also wrote several more Masses and other sacred works. But what really interested him was opera – and in the summer of 1780 he received the commission he had been waiting for.

*The title page of a score of* Idomeneo

He was asked to write a new opera for Munich, for the 1781 Carnival season (the period of festivity in some European countries between the end of the Christmas season and the beginning of Lent). The chosen subject was the Greek legend of Idomeneus, King of Crete, who is caught in a storm at sea on his way home, and vows that if he is spared, he will sacrifice to Neptune (god of the sea) the first human being he meets on dry land. This, of course, turns out to be his own son. But, in the tradition of the time, the opera manages to have a happy ending, suitable for the Carnival season.

*Idomeneo* is Mozart's first really great opera, the first time he was able to demonstrate his amazing talent for allowing cardboard characters to express real human emotions – joy, grief, rage, suffering – through the medium of music. It was this talent – which Mozart possessed to a far higher degree than most, if not all, of his contemporaries – which marked him out from them as a uniquely gifted composer. The result is that his music is as real and vivid now as it was when it was first written, 200 years ago.

# 4  Vienna: Early Years

Still basking in the glow of success, Wolfgang and his family took advantage of the Archbishop's absence to relax in the Carnival atmosphere of Munich. Among the pieces he wrote there was the delightful Piano Sonata in A major, with its famous "Turkish Rondo" finale.

But on March 12, 1781, Wolfgang was peremptorily summoned to Vienna by the Archbishop, who had gone there for the celebrations marking the accession of the new Emperor, Joseph II. Wolfgang was to join the Archbishop there immediately, and there his humiliating position became even more intolerable: he was made to eat with the servants, and was forbidden to give concerts, except at the Archbishop's request. That way he was denied the chance to make extra money: he was particularly annoyed when the Archbishop forbade him to play at one concert in the Emperor's presence, at which he could have made half a year's salary in a single evening.

The antagonism between Wolfgang and the Archbishop soon reached boiling point. Colloredo refused to let Wolfgang stay on for a few extra days, and ordered him home.

After a stormy interview, during which both parties lost their tempers, Wolfgang resigned and was unceremoniously booted out with a "box on the ear and a kick on the backside."

His intention, then, was to stay in Vienna, making a living as a freelance musician by giving concerts, composing when required, and teaching. This was an incredibly bold move, and, although he could not have foreseen it, Wolfgang chose exactly the wrong time to do it.

Unless a composer was attached to a private patron, or to a court, the only way to make money from his craft was to sell his compositions to a publisher or a private individual who would pay enough for them. In those days, there were no copyright laws or performance rights, so once a piece of music was freely available, anyone could copy or print it to sell, or perform it without benefit to the composer. Sixty years after Mozart died, the German composer Gustav Lortzing literally starved to death, having been forced to sell his hugely successful operas to a publisher for a pitifully small outright fee.

## "Turkish Rondo" from the Piano Sonata in A major

*The Mozart family in the winter of 1780–81*

As a performer, Mozart hoped to make a living from giving concerts. When he first arrived in Vienna, there were plenty of opportunities: many rich aristocrats supported their own private orchestras, and the music-loving Viennese were always ready to hear new talent. Many of these concerts, which often took place in the city's theaters during periods such as Lent when the theaters were officially closed, were supported by private subscribers, who put up the money in advance. But during the 1780s, Austria was engaged in a long and wearying war against the Turkish Empire – which accounts for the then contemporary obsession with "Turkish" fashions and customs – and within a few years many people's purses had been emptied by the war effort. As Mozart was to find to his cost, economic circumstances were not very favorable to the struggling musician without a secure job and a steady income, and, by the end of his life, he could not find enough subscribers to raise the money to put concerts on. He did have a few wealthy pupils, but he was far too talented a player and composer to want to devote all his time to teaching.

Mozart's tragedy was that he stood at a crossroads in history: the feudal values of a dying century were about to give way to a new age, in which ordinary people (not just rich aristocrats) would enjoy new freedoms and a higher standard of living, while artists would gradually be appreciated in their own right, and not just treated as mere craftsmen or servants. Nonetheless, Mozart's career certainly broke the mold of the old patronage system, and, as the Age of Enlightenment began to replace the old regime, artists such as Beethoven (who was a better businessman than Mozart) were able to turn the new climate to their advantage.

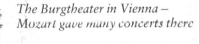

*The Burgtheater in Vienna – Mozart gave many concerts there*

25

Leopold Mozart – a typical product of the old regime in his constant anxiety to secure a good job for Wolfgang – was deeply worried about his son's decision. And worse was to come. Wolfgang had taken up lodgings with the Weber family. Although Aloysia was now married and working as a singer in Vienna, old Madame Weber was a born schemer. She had failed to make a match between Wolfgang and Aloysia, but she had other daughters. One of these was the nineteen-year-old Constanze, not such a good singer as her elder sister, but agreeable, attractive, and fond of music. Within a few months, people were gossiping about Wolfgang's friendship with Constanze – which Madame Weber did nothing to discourage – and by Christmas 1781 he was asking for Leopold's blessing on their marriage. "Constanze is the family martyr," he wrote to Leopold, "the kindest-natured, the cleverest, and the best of all of them . . . She is not ugly, but she is no beauty either. Her best features are two little black eyes and a nice figure. She is not witty, but she has enough common sense to make an excellent wife and mother. I love her and she loves me with all her heart. Tell me whether I could ask for a better wife?"

Leopold was appalled. How was Wolfgang going to support himself, let alone a wife and family? He had a few piano pupils, to be sure, including the ugly but talented Josepha von Auernhammer, for whom he wrote some piano music; several concerts were lined up, and he was selling a few pieces to Viennese publishers, but Leopold knew that wouldn't be enough. However, Wolfgang was determined: two could live as cheaply as one, he told his father. By the end of July 1782, he decided not to wait any longer for Leopold's permission – which technically he did not need anyway, being over twenty-one – and he and Constanze were married on August 4, at St. Stephen's Cathedral.

*Constanze Mozart (1762–1842), painted by her brother-in-law, Joseph Lange*

*St. Stephen's Cathedral in Vienna, where Wolfgang and Constanze were married*

Leopold's grudging blessing arrived by post the next day. The marriage was very happy – but Leopold never forgave his son.

During his engagement, Wolfgang had occupied himself with writing a new opera, *Die Entführung aus dem Serail* (The flight from the harem), whose heroine was also called Constanze. It was a comic opera with spoken dialogue in German (a Singspiel), and the plot concerned the efforts of two young men to rescue their sweethearts from a Turkish harem. It was Mozart's most ambitious comic opera so far, and it should have been a brilliant success – but for the fact that the Emperor, who came to the first performance, remarked to Mozart afterwards that it seemed to have "too many notes." "Just as many as it needs, Your Majesty," Wolfgang is said to have replied. But it did have a good run of twenty performances, and it made Wolfgang 1200 florins (over $4000 in today's money) in the first two days.

Mozart wrote a great deal of music during his first year in Vienna. Apart from the opera, he composed the "Haffner" Symphony for the Haffner family in Salzburg; three magnificent wind serenades; three piano concertos to play himself at his concerts; and an unfinished Mass in C minor, begun as an act of thanksgiving for his marriage.

In January 1783 Mozart and Constanze moved into a new flat, which was big enough for them to hold a New Year's party. On June 17, their first child was born – a boy named Raimund Leopold after his godfather and his grandfather. Only six weeks later, Wolfgang and Constanze set out for Salzburg to visit Leopold, leaving the baby behind with a nurse. Not surprisingly, he died while they were away.

We do not know how Leopold got on with his daughter-in-law, whom he mistrusted, but the visit can't have been particularly relaxed. After three months, Wolf-

*Mozart at the time of his marriage; an unfinished portrait by Joseph Lange*

27

gang and Constanze went back to Vienna by way of the city of Linz, where Mozart dashed off a new symphony – named after the city – for a concert. The next year, 1784, was his best and happiest. He and his wife got on well together, except for a constant shortage of money. They liked to entertain their many friends, and to dress well and keep their own carriage – all of which was expensive. But Mozart had a busy teaching and concert program – during five weeks in Lent he gave nineteen concerts altogether, for which he wrote several fine new piano concertos.

In September Constanze had a second son, christened Carl Thomas. He lived to the ripe old age of seventy-four; but the Mozarts were to lose three more babies before they produced another surviving child, not long before Wolfgang's own death.

*Mozart's two surviving children, Carl and Franz Xaver, in 1798*

28

# 5  Vienna: Last Years

In December 1784 Wolfgang joined the Freemasons. This powerful movement, with its origins in medieval societies, had quickly spread all over Europe in the eighteenth century, and was especially strong in England, France, and Austria. Its aims were to promote idealistic philosophies, including the notion that all men were brothers. Although its membership included many rich and powerful men, it was beginning to be looked upon as potentially dangerous by Europe's rulers. If all men were to be equal, no throne would be safe. In Austria the new Emperor, Joseph II, was particularly worried, and his secret police kept a close watch on the activities of the Masons. A year after Mozart joined, Joseph ordered the number of Viennese lodges to be cut down to three, and many were closed or amalgamated.

Mozart's membership of the Freemasons was to have far-reaching effects on the rest of his life. He may well have joined largely for its material benefits, thinking it a useful way up the social ladder, and as he ran into financial difficulties, he found he could turn to his brother Masons – who are obliged to help each other out when in distress – for loans of cash to tide him over. In return, he wrote music for various Masonic functions, but the most important musical result, as we shall see, was the creation of his last opera, *The Magic Flute*.

In the spring of 1785 Leopold paid his son a visit, and

*The Emperor Joseph II, who ruled Austria 1781–90*

*A meeting of Mozart's Masonic Lodge in Vienna*

*Mozart's piano*

his life, Leopold must have been content. But when he left to go home, neither he nor Wolfgang knew that they had seen each other for the last time. Leopold died, alone and embittered, two years later.

Wolfgang's reputation was beginning to spread: his music was being published, and his operas were performed all over Germany and Austria. By the end of the year he had begun work on a daring new operatic venture – a setting of the notorious French play *The Marriage of Figaro*, which had been banned in Vienna by the Emperor the previous year for its outspoken attack on aristocratic morals. The man who adapted the text (the "librettist") was an Italian adventurer, ex-priest and poet called Lorenzo da Ponte, whose

*Lorenzo da Ponte (1749–1838)*

was much impressed by Wolfgang's standard of living, and by his apparent success. His concerts were full, and were attended by the aristocracy, sometimes even by the Emperor himself. "We drove to Wolfgang's first subscription concert, at which many members of the aristocracy were present," Leopold proudly wrote to Nannerl in Salzburg. "The concert was wonderful, and the orchestra played brilliantly."

Wolfgang was also writing marvelous new works, including two more piano concertos full of passion, drama, and beauty. The great Joseph Haydn, to whom Wolfgang had dedicated a set of his finest string quartets, told Leopold to his face that his son was the greatest composer he knew "either personally or by reputation. He has taste, and what is more, the most profound knowledge of composition . . ." Constanze seemed to be managing the household economically, and the money appeared to be flowing in. For once in

own life had been full of scandal. Da Ponte and Mozart later collaborated on two more brilliant comic operas. _Figaro_, _Don Giovanni_ and _Così fan tutte_ are all regarded as masterpieces, and are all regularly performed today.

Mozart and da Ponte slightly simplified the complicated plot of _Figaro_, which concerns the efforts of the wily valet Figaro and his fiancée Susanna to get married. To do so, they have to outwit their master, the Count, who has fallen out of love with his own wife, and has his eye on the pretty Susanna. The opera contains a number of popular tunes which were instant hits – such as Figaro's song which ends the first act.

## _"Non più andrai" from "The Marriage of Figaro"_

*Nancy Storace (1765–1817) the first Susanna in* Figaro

*A page of Mozart's C minor Piano Concerto (Mozart drew little heads on the music)*

But for all its quicksilver wit and masterly music, *Figaro* was not a great success in Vienna. Other composers, including the powerful court composer Antonio Salieri, were intensely jealous of Mozart's talent, and they did everything possible to sabotage its performances. Mozart was finding life increasingly hard without a regular income. He was still writing concertos for his concerts, but there were fewer of these. In October 1786 he seriously considered packing up and going to England to make some money. Unfortunately, Leopold refused to look after the two children – Carl and a new baby Johann (who lived only for a month).

Life improved early in 1787, when Mozart was invited to the Bohemian capital of Prague, where *Figaro* had been put on with enormous success. The whole city had gone quite "Figaro-mad," and everyone was singing or dancing to the catchy tunes. Mozart and Constanze thoroughly enjoyed their visit, for which Wolfgang wrote a new symphony, the "Prague." And, most importantly, he was asked to write a

new opera for the following autumn. This was *Don Giovanni*, the tale of a swashbuckling adventurer and womanizer, who kills the father of one of his victims in a duel, is haunted by the murdered man's ghost, and is eventually dragged down to Hell when he refuses to make amends. Not exactly suitable subject matter for a comic opera! It was nevertheless a great hit in Prague; and while he was working on it, Mozart took time off to write some chamber music, including the exquisite serenade *Eine kleine Nachtmusik*.

IL DISSOLUTO PUNITO
ossia
IL DON GIOVANNI
Dramma giocoso in due Atti
posto in Musica da
*Wolfgang Amadeus Mozart*

Ridotto per il Pianoforte da A. E. Müller
presso Breitkopf e Härtel in Lipsia.
Pr. 4 Rthlr.

*A view of Prague*

*The title page of a score of* Don Giovanni

34

## Romanze from "Eine kleine Nachtmusik" for string quartet

When he returned to Vienna, he found an unexpected surprise. He had at last been given a formal appointment at the Viennese court – as chamber composer. The salary was not much (800 florins – about $2,700 in today's money), but it was a regular income, and all he had to do was to write dance music for the court balls. This was good news: the Mozarts were desperately short of cash and had been forced to leave their fashionable flat in central Vienna for a smaller and cheaper one. In December 1787 they moved again, just before Constanze had another baby – this time a daughter, who lived for only six months.

By June 1788, Mozart was writing begging letters almost every day to his brother Freemasons. He and Constanze moved house again – to an even cheaper suburb, where Wolfgang wrote his three last and finest symphonies – 39, 40, and 41 (the "Jupiter") – all within the space of a few weeks. In May, *Don Giovanni* was performed in Vienna, but it was even less successful than *Figaro* had been. To earn a little extra money, Mozart – the most creative composer of his time – was reduced to making arrangements of other composers' music, especially by Bach and Handel.

*Mozart in April 1789, by Doris Stock*

*The Graben, a street in Vienna where Mozart lived for a while*

## Opening of the Symphony No.40 in G minor

38

In April 1789 Wolfgang visited Berlin, where he met the King, Frederick II, and gave a few concerts – but he did not make any money, and he hated being separated from Constanze. "Dearest little wife, if only I had a letter from you," he wrote affectionately to her. "If I was to tell you all the things I do with your dear portrait, it would make you laugh. For instance, when I take it out of its case, I say 'Hello Stanzerl! Hello little scamp, kitten-face, little button nose, little trifle, Schluck-und-Druck . . .' O Stru! Stri! I kiss you 1095060437082 times and am your most faithful husband and friend, Wolfgang!"

In the summer, both he and Constanze fell seriously ill, and Mozart was unable to work. But his friend and fellow-Mason Michael Puchberg, a wealthy merchant, came to his rescue and loaned Mozart enough money to send his wife to the spa at Baden, a few miles outside Vienna. She spent a good deal of time there over the next two years, taking the waters and indulging in a few mild flirtations, which made Mozart jealous.

In the autumn Mozart was asked to write another comic opera, once more with Da Ponte. *Così fan tutte* (They're all the same) had a tongue-in-cheek story about two young men who are persuaded to test their girlfriends' faithfulness – with disastrous results (the girls eventually fall for each other's boyfriends, who woo them in disguise). Although the opera was much more popular than the last two, the Emperor unfortunately died shortly after the first performance, and all the theatres were closed while the court was in mourning.

In September 1790 Mozart decided to visit Frankfurt for the new Emperor's coronation as Holy Roman Emperor of the Germans. He hoped to gain notice – but Leopold II had other things to think about, and Mozart found himself among a crowd of similar attention-seekers. Although he

gave a few concerts, he made little money from them, and he returned home deeply depressed. "Everything seems as cold as ice to me," he wrote to Constanze.

1791 was Mozart's last year. Over the spring he busied himself with writing a lot of small pieces – dance music, pieces for mechanical organ and glass harmonica (both fashionable toys at the time) and his last piano concerto, a rather serious, melancholy work, with none of the joyful exuberance of the earlier concertos. Many of these were published, and Mozart earned quite a lot of money from them. His financial position seems to have improved, and in the spring and early summer he felt better and more cheerful than he had for some time.

In June, Constanze went to Baden as usual, where she had her last child, a boy called Franz Xaver. He was to become a good pianist, like his father, but a rather poor composer. Meanwhile, Wolfgang was enjoying himself with

Emanuel Schikaneder as Papageno
in The Magic Flute

1785–1791

40

his friends, and one of these, an actor/manager and amateur singer and fellow-Freemason, Emanuel Schikaneder, suggested to Mozart that he should write an opera for the theatre which Schikaneder ran in the suburbs. This was to be *The Magic Flute* (Die Zauberflöte), an opera in German with spoken dialogue (known as a Singspiel). It had a rather silly story – more like a pantomime than a real opera. Prince Tamino is asked by the Queen of the Night to rescue her lovely daughter Pamina from the clutches of a wicked magician called Sarastro, and is given some magic instruments – a flute and a set of bells – to help him. But Sarastro turns out to be a wise and good man, who has taken Pamina away from her evil mother for her own good, in order that she may eventually marry Tamino. The opera contains some of Mozart's most appealing and tuneful music, especially the song for the birdcatcher, Papageno (who was played by Schikaneder himself).

## Papageno's song from "The Magic Flute"

**Andante**

(Papageno's whistle)

41

*The title-page of the printed text of* The Magic Flute, *showing the Masonic symbols of the trowel, compasses and five-pointed star*

But anyone who looked more closely would realize that the opera is more than just an amusing pantomime with delightful music. In it, Mozart revealed on stage thinly-disguised versions of some of the most secret Masonic rites and initiation ceremonies – something all Masons were forbidden to do on pain of death – and the whole piece is full of Masonic symbolism, including the magic number three. It has even been suggested that the evil Queen of the Night was meant to be the former Empress, Maria Theresia, and that Sarastro represented a famous scientist and thinker who was Grand Master of one of the Viennese Lodges. *The Magic Flute* was, in fact, a Masonic opera. Why did Mozart do it? Some people say that the Masons had him killed in revenge for betraying their secrets – but Schikaneder, who was just as guilty, got away scot-free. Another theory is that because Freemasonry was under threat, Mozart wanted to present it publicly as a noble and good society, with high-minded and virtuous aims, in order to protect it from destruction by the new Emperor. If so, he failed: the movement was to be wiped out in Austria within three years.

1785–1791

PAMINA *Du hier !* — *Güttige Götter* =
*Achzehenter Auftritt. II. Act.*

*A scene from a 1793 production of* The Magic Flute

*A page of Mozart's own catalog of his works*

While he was working on *The Magic Flute*, Mozart was asked to write two more pieces of music. One was another opera, for the coronation in Prague of the new Emperor as King of Bohemia. Mozart had exactly eighteen days to write the whole piece – a rather artificial concoction, suitable for the occasion, called *La clemenza di Tito* (The clemency of Titus), about an ancient Roman emperor who generously pardons his enemies. In fact, he wrote most of it on the stagecoach to Prague. *Tito* was the kind of opera that was already thought to be boring and old-fashioned, and though it served its purpose, it was not a success.

The other piece was something of a mystery. The story has it that a stranger, dressed in gray, appeared one day and asked Mozart, on behalf of an unnamed patron, to write a Requiem Mass, for which he would be handsomely paid. Mozart agreed to take on the job, but he was not allowed to ask who wanted it. In fact, the commission came from a

*The apartment where Mozart died on the Rauhensteingasse, Vienna*

Viennese nobleman who enjoyed paying composers to write pieces anonymously, and then passing them off as his own work. He wanted the Requiem as a memorial to his beautiful young wife, who had recently died. But Mozart knew nothing of this, and as the autumn wore on and his health

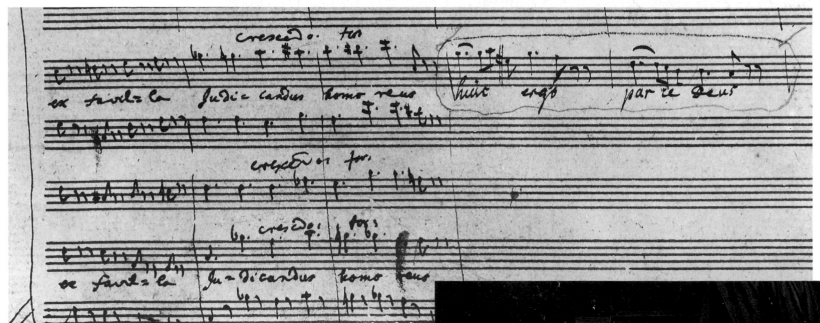

*The last page of music Mozart wrote, from the unfinished* Requiem

worsened, the Requiem began to prey on his mind, and he became convinced that it would be for himself.

In the late autumn, the weather changed for the worse, and in the wintry conditions Mozart fell seriously ill again. He was certain that he was being poisoned by his enemies (he was suffering from high fevers and violent stomach pains); in fact he had advanced kidney disease, and nothing could have saved him. Desperate to finish the Requiem, he struggled on, but soon he was forced to take to his bed. On Monday, December 5, 1791, at one o' clock in the morning, he died in his wife's arms. He was buried the next day, after a service at St. Stephen's Cathedral, at a cemetery an hour's walk from the city. Because Constanze had very little money, he had the cheapest possible funeral, and his body was buried in an unmarked grave.

*Mozart's death*

Mozart's lasting memorial, however, is not a name on a weather-beaten tombstone, but over 600 pieces of the marvelously fresh and alive music which two centuries later is still treasured by musicians and music lovers all over the world. Through this music the name of Wolfgang Amadeus Mozart – the composer truly "beloved of God" – will live as long as civilization itself.

*Mozart's memorial in Vienna*

sinfonia concerta

# Glossary of Musical Terms

**Opera** A play set to music, usually in several acts. Most eighteenth-century operas were sung in Italian.

**Aria** A song, usually from an opera, in Italian.

**Singspiel** "Song-play." An opera in German, not Italian, with spoken dialogue between the songs.

**Minuet** A courtly, graceful dance, much used for short piano pieces, or as one section of a larger orchestral piece.

**Sonata** A piece for one or two instruments (such as piano alone, or violin and piano) in several sections (called "movements").

**Symphony** A large-scale orchestral piece, usually in four separate sections (movements). The first and last were usually quick; the second slow, and the third was often a minuet (see above).

**Concerto** A piece often in three movements for a solo instrument and orchestra, intended to show off the soloist's technique. The most common concertos were for piano or violin, but Mozart wrote some for wind instruments, too. The first and third movements were fast, and the middle one slow.

**Sinfonia Concertante** "Concerted symphony." A cross between concerto and symphony, for two or more solo instruments.

**Serenade** A piece for instruments or orchestra in many movements, intended to be played out of doors for evening entertainment.

**Chamber Music** Pieces for a small, but varied group of instruments, each playing an individual part.

**Duet** A piece for 2 instruments.

**Trio** A piece of chamber music for 3 instruments.

**Quartet** A piece of chamber music for 4 instruments (a string quartet consisted of 2 violins, viola and cello).

**Quintet** A piece of chamber music for 5 instruments.

**Mass** A musical setting of the Catholic service, in Latin, for church use.

**Requiem** A musical setting of the Latin Mass for the Dead.

# List of Works

Mozart wrote over 600 pieces of music, in the following categories:

## Operas

20, including *Idomeneo* (1781), *Die Entführung aus dem Serail* (1782), *Le Nozze di Figaro* (1786), *Don Giovanni* (1787), *Così fan tutte* (1790), *Die Zauberflöte* (1791), *La Clemenza di Tito* (1791).

## Vocal Music

Around 55 concert arias for voice and orchestra, around 30 songs for voice and piano, 15 songs for more than one voice with orchestra or piano. Many canons and rounds.

## Sacred Music

17 Masses; 1 Requiem (unfinished), vespers, litanies, antiphons and motets.

## Symphonies

48, including the "Paris" (1778), the "Haffner" (1782), the "Linz" (1783), the "Prague" (1786), the E flat, the G minor and the "Jupiter" (all 1788).

## Serenades

21 for mixed wind and string instruments, including the "Haffner" (1776), the "Posthorn" (1779), *Eine Kleine Nachtmusik* (1787). 17 for wind instruments, including the Serenades in B flat (1781), E flat (1781), and C minor (1782/3).

## Dance Music for Orchestra

Around 103 minuets, 56 German dances, 36 country dances.

## Concertos

23 for piano, 5 for violin, 1 for 2 violins, 1 for violin and viola, 1 for bassoon, 1 for flute, 1 for oboe or flute, 1 for flute and harp, 4 for horn, 1 for clarinet.

## Chamber Music

4 flute quartets, 1 oboe quartet, 1 horn quintet, 1 clarinet quintet, 6 string quintets, 26 string quartets, 1 string trio, 7 piano trios, 2 piano quartets, 1 piano quintet, 1 trio for piano, clarinet and viola, 36 sonatas for violin and piano, 3 pieces for mechanical organ, 2 pieces for glass harmonica.

## Solo Piano Music

18 sonatas, 5 sonatas for piano duet, 1 sonata for 2 pianos, 16 sets of variations, 1 set of variations for piano duet, around 40 miscellaneous pieces for solo piano.

VIKING
Published by the Penguin Group
Viking Penguin, a division of Penguin Books USA Inc., 375 Hudson Street, New York, New York 10014, U.S.A.
Penguin Books Ltd, 27 Wrights Lane, London W8 5TZ, England
Penguin Books Australia Ltd, Ringwood, Victoria, Australia
Penguin Books Canada Ltd, 2801 John Street, Markham, Ontario, Canada L3R 1B4
Penguin Books (N.Z.) Ltd, 182–190 Wairau Road, Auckland 10, New Zealand

Penguin Books Ltd, Registered Offices: Harmondsworth, Middlesex, England

First published in Great Britain by Faber & Faber Ltd in association with Faber Music Ltd, 1990

First American edition published in 1991
10 9 8 7 6 5 4 3 2

ISBN 0-670-83679-6
CIP data available upon request

Printed in Spain by Mateu Cromo, Madrid